T0245759

ALSO BY BRIT BARRON

*Worth It: Overcome Your Fears and Embrace
the Life You Were Made For*

DO YOU STILL TALK TO GRANDMA?

WORKBOOK

DO YOU STILL TALK TO GRANDMA?

WORKBOOK

When the Problematic
People in Our Lives Are
the Ones We Love

BRIT BARRON

CONVERGENT
NEW YORK

Copyright © 2024 by Brit Barron

Illustrations: Adobe Stock/Racer57 (page 28), Adobe Stock/Mark Rasmussen (page 28), Adobe Stock/korkeng (pages 29, 30).

All rights reserved.

Published in the United States by Convergent Books,
an imprint of Random House, a division of
Penguin Random House LLC, New York.

CONVERGENT BOOKS is a registered trademark and the Convergent colophon is a trademark of Penguin Random House LLC.

ISBN 978-0-593-59437-7
Ebook ISBN 978-0-593-59438-4

This work is based on and directly quotes *Do You Still Talk to Grandma?* by Brit Barron, first published by Convergent Books, an imprint of Random House, a division of Penguin Random House LLC, in 2024, copyright © 2024 by Brit Barron.

Printed in the United States of America on acid-free paper

convergentbooks.com

2 4 6 8 9 7 5 3 1

First Edition

Book design by Susan Turner

CONTENTS

INTRODUCTION

WELCOME TO THE *DO YOU STILL TALK TO GRANDMA? Workbook*. This is meant to be your guide in the movement away from the internet, away from the arguments with strangers, and toward our common goal: progress, healing, evolution. This is such a unique time we are living in because we are the only people in history who have ever had this much access to endless information and endless opportunity for connecting with people. But how do we make it work for us and not against us? We've all been there. We all know the feeling of waking up in the middle of the night or first thing in the morning, waiting in line at the store, sitting bored at home, watching TV, avoiding our own emotional distress, and then what do we do? We reach for our phones. We try to fill every gap in our lives with more information or more two-dimensional connection. But we need to take a step back, put the phone down, take in the world around us, and assess how we think and feel about it—how we are finding our place in it and how it is shaping us.

We are in control of ourselves if we want to be. We are not bound to the narratives that we are handed, and we are not held captive to the loudest voices. In fact, in a world with millions of voices speaking at the same time, the most radical thing you can do is listen to yourself. This workbook is an invitation to do just that. Let's turn down the noise, take a step back, and look at the world around us. Let's dig deep inside ourselves and come out on the other side. Let's make ourselves ready to hold complexity and nuance and stop letting external authorities guide our lives and ideas. Let's get back in the driver's seat. Let's chart our own path forward. Let's find healing and transformation, and truly—if nothing else—let's stop arguing with strangers on the internet.

DO YOU STILL TALK TO GRANDMA?

WORKBOOK

1

Moving Beyond Heroes and Villains

NONE OF US ARE STRANGERS TO BINARY THINKING. IT has filled every corner of our understanding of the world since we were babies. I can tell you every Disney movie I saw and their heroes and villains. *The Lion King* was the first movie I ever saw at the drive-in movie theater, and I'll never forget when Scar came on-screen; I immediately knew he was the villain. The way he walked, the way he looked—my little mind had already been trained to look for the villain, identify the problem, the bad guy, and then, of course, to find the hero, support them, cheer for them, root them on in their journey of overcoming the villain.

You know the feeling, right? There are Disney heroes and Disney villains.

Let's take a closer look at a few. Write down your favorites in the columns below:

DISNEY HEROES   **DISNEY VILLAINS**

....

....

....

....

....

OK, now that we've got our brains warmed up on some good ol' Disney characters, let's do the same activity but this time with historical figures. Write down absolutely anyone from history you think would fall into the hero or villain category:

HISTORICAL HEROES   **HISTORICAL VILLAINS**

....

....

....

....

....

How did that feel? Was it difficult? Was it easy? I would wager that for most of us, unless you've never seen a Disney movie, in which case this was probably very difficult, both of these lists were fairly easy to populate. We know the heroes and villains of the stories we watched growing up, and we know the heroes and villains of our history. Our brains already know how to split and divide people into one of two very clean and tidy categories. But what happens when we live in a world where the lines and categories aren't that clean or tidy?

Part of us can't help but make these lines and distinctions. We desire and tend toward binary thinking and polarization because of a psychological experience known as "splitting."

Psychoanalyst Melanie Klein defined this form of psychic functioning—splitting the world into good or bad, friends or foes, "like" and "do not like"—as the "paranoid-schizoid position." We can fall into this position in times of stress, and it explains our tendency to consider differences not simply as variations but as opposites.

In what ways does this feel relatable? When was a time you were so stressed that you just needed something to make sense?

....

....

....

....

....

....

When was a time you were so stressed that you saw differences as opposite—that you saw variation as a threat?

....

....

....

....

....

....

....

Let's take a further look at this. I want you to think back to 2020 (I know, trauma). That year was a time of massive collective stress.

What variation did you see in 2020 that you felt was an opposing side?

....

....

....

....

....

....

....

I'll give you an example from my own experience.

Armed with the most minimal amount of information early in the pandemic, everyone was wearing all sorts of masks. I remember at one point I was walking around with a headband that I had filled with a coffee filter. It was chaos. But eventually, people started selling masks and making more masks, and soon after that, in my heightened stress, I started making a lot of judgments about people who simply tied bandanas around their mouths. This felt like more than a variation; this was an opposition. My brain was in peak splitting mode, and anytime I saw someone with a bandana mask, I felt, "They don't care about people, they don't care about me, I bet I know who they voted for, they are a villain."

You see how that works? What could be seen as a variation was now seen as opposition because my brain was *stressed*.

Where did your brain go in 2020? What binary lines did you draw? Who were your 2020 villains?

....

....

....

....

....

....

The problem with binary thinking, aside from the way it can cause us to treat people, is the reality that it's just not factually true. I had no idea why any of those people had bandana masks. Maybe they didn't have access to buy other masks; maybe they were running out of the house and that was the only one they could find; maybe they were on their way to buy a new mask; maybe they had a coffee filter in it (literally like me the week before); maybe they were actually mean and hated people and didn't care. But whatever the case, there was nuance, and that nuance is important.

In *Do You Still Talk to Grandma?* I tell the story of the Good Samaritan. A man was beaten down in the road, and two people simply passed him by until a third man stopped to help him. Moral of the story? Be the third guy, right? Well, I think the point of the story is that we will at some time find ourselves as every character in the story. And if we can begin to hold that nuance for ourselves, we can hold it for the world around us.

So let's give this a try together.

I invite you to think about your own life and write about these moments—and really sit with these and remember how each one felt.

A time you were heartbroken:

....

....

....

....

....

A time you broke a heart:

....

....

....

....

....

....

....

A time you helped someone in need:

....

....

....

....

....

....

....

A time you did nothing:

....

....

....

....

....

....

....

A time you felt proud:

....

....

....

....

....

....

A moment you regret:

....

....

....

....

....

....

Thank you for your honesty.

Now, we could go on and on, right? We look at our lives and we see mountains and valleys. We see roses and thorns, moments where we play the hero, and moments where we play the villain, and they're all wrapped into one whole person. So what does that mean? Which is it? Are we good or bad? Hero or villain? Or are we invited to a life of holding all of the nuance of our experience that shapes who we are and how we move through the world?

Now go deeper: Why did you do the thing you regret? What reason did you have for breaking someone's heart? What was happening in you that spilled out into the people around you?

....

....

....

....

....

....

....

Now let's take it even further.

Which of your regrets or times you broke someone's heart outweigh the times you showed up? Stepped up?

....

....

....

....

....

....

....

Let's get personal. I want you to think of someone in your life that you have put in a binary, or a person that you have a hard time finding nuance for. In *Do You Still Talk to Grandma?* I use a fairly common example of my gay friend and his homophobic grandma.

Who is your person and what did they do that made you put them in a binary role?

....

....

....

....

....

....

List all the things that you love about them:

....

....

....

....

....

....

What is your favorite memory with them?

....

....

....

....

....

....

....

OK, now list all the ways they have disappointed you:

....

....

....

....

....

....

....

How have they hurt you?

....

....

....

....

....

....

....

Knowing that all of this is true, what do we do now? I wish it were a perfect equation. I wish I could tell you that if you have fifteen good memories and three disappointments, then the person gets to stay in your life. Or that if they only hurt you at a level of 6.5/10 or lower, then you can still go to Thanksgiving at their house.

The goal is not to find a magical equation; the goal is first to be able to hold our own nuance, and then to begin to hold it for others.

The people of X (formerly Twitter) do not get to make the final call on whether or not the above person (or any person) gets to stay in your life.

Which brings us to external authorities.

Beyond our binary thinking, another factor that can make it difficult to hold nuance for the people in our lives is the presence of and desire for external authorities.

It's always funny to me how many of my friends have left the church only to make Brené Brown their new pastor (no shade to Brené—I am a huge fan). There is something comforting about a person who gets onstage every Sunday or who releases a podcast every Tuesday that you can trust will have the answers for you. We love having someone else tell us what to do or what to think and feel.

Besides your parents, who are some of the external authorities you grew up with (pastors, coaches, teachers, etc.)?

....

....

....

....

....

....

The added twist of living in our current time is that because everyone has a microphone (quite literally), our search for an external authority doesn't even need to leave the palm of our hand.

Describe your favorite influencers you follow on social media:

....

....

....

....

....

....

....

....

....

Now, here's the tricky part. We all have relationships that require us to do our own work, find the nuance that makes sense for us, and set appropriate boundaries (more on that later), but what happens when our favorite fitness influencer tells us, "No matter what, if you still have a relationship with a homophobic family member, then you deserve to be blocked"?

What happens when we have literally thousands of micro external authorities screaming in our ears telling us how we should handle the nuance of our own lives?

When did an external authority lead you to do something you later regretted?

....

....

....

....

....

....

....

....

Our ability to hold nuance for and boundaries with external authorities is absolutely essential if we want to find a new way forward.

2

Internet Brain

WHEN I WAS IN MY TWENTIES AND PASSING AS A straight woman, I can't tell you how many times I pretended to like football. It was doubly difficult because not only was I pretending to be attracted to men in general, but I was also pretending to like their interests.

In *Do You Still Talk to Grandma?* I share a story about a man who was at a flat-earther conference and admitted that he didn't have much interest at all in the shape of the earth; this was just a way for him to make friends.

What lies have you told to be part of a group? What have you pretended to like for the sake of someone else, such as someone you were dating?

....

....

....

....

....

....

....

....

We do this because our desire for community and connection is one of our strongest driving forces as humans.

As we get older, it can be hard to recount all of our experiences in life, but let's see how quickly you can remember things about your very first best friend.

What was their name? What were they like? What did you do together?

....

....

....

....

....

....

....

....

My first best friend's name was Crystal, and I could tell you many things about our time as friends before my family moved to a different state.

I remember Crystal clearly; I remember how simple that friendship was, how easy it was. And I also remember my middle school friendships. I remember the desperation to stay as a part of the group of friends that I had made. I pretended to be interested in things they were interested in. I knew it would be easier to pretend I thought a stupid movie was funny than it would be to go through middle school without friends.

What are the first memories that come to your mind when you think of middle school friendships?

....

....

....

....

....

....

....

....

I remember being in middle school and judging my every move based on whether I thought it would support or diminish my sense of community.

I was in a constant state of embarrassment alert—

making sure nothing I said or did could put me in the absolute unforgiving presence of the middle school jury.

Can you relate?

What was your biggest fear in middle school?

....

....

....

....

....

....

....

....

I eventually grew up and those feelings subsided. I still desperately want and need community, but I am a lot less likely to lie to be a part of it. If a movie isn't funny, I'm not laughing. If I don't like something, I'll say it. I am a fully grown mature adult, right?

Wrong.

Something about the constant threat of critique on the internet brings me more middle school flashbacks than I had watching the movie *Mean Girls* for the first time.

The external authorities on social media are not afraid to tell you exactly what they think of you, and your presence and belonging in a group is never secure. That sense of community you feel being a part of the _____ internet community is under constant watch for a breach of the unspoken but absolutely inviolable rules.

What online community or communities do you feel part of? What have you done to stay in the good graces of their members?

....

....

....

....

....

....

....

....

I have spent a lot of my life in antiracism work and would definitely consider myself a liberal progressive person, and in recent years my middle school self has been front and center as I find myself wanting to self-censor, but also to do the thing that will keep me in my community's good graces.

Here's my example.

On June 25, 2021, the news broke that Derek Chauvin had been found guilty for the murder of George Floyd. It was a murder that had poured gasoline on the flames of antiracist movements all over America and the world. George Floyd's life, and absolutely unwarranted death, sparked conversations, books, protests, and vigils. You were there; you saw it. It was a turning point for so many of us that I think we all wish could have come by any other means. The reality that a life (and not only his) had to be lost to get our attention anchored the whole racial justice movement in tragedy. But one thing was for sure—George Floyd's murderer was guilty, and we all knew it because we all saw it. We watched on our phones, we held that story in our hands, and we knew. Still, this country does not have a strong history when it comes to justice for Black lives, and a lot of people, myself included, doubted that we would see Chauvin held accountable.

But after a summer of revolution, on June 25 the next year, accountability came, and here's what happened: I was living in my middle school mind. There was constant critique from all angles of the progressives on the internet, and I remember sitting there, learning that George Floyd's murderer had been found guilty, and before I could even formulate my own thoughts or feelings . . . I ran to my phone and frantically opened up Instagram and started posting on my story. I had to say something. I had to let my group know I was still there, still deserving of their connection. But what should I say? How could I say it so that they wouldn't critique me

or kick me out of their club? What was the right response to keep my connection intact?

"Guilty" with praise hand emojis?

No, just "guilty."

No, say something more meaningful, something deeper . . .

Talk about what you are feeling.

Wait, what am I feeling?

*I think I know what I'm feeling, but let me see what other
people are saying first to see if what I'm feeling is right.*

I looked at the profile of someone I admire.

"We shouldn't be celebrating. George Floyd should
still be alive," they posted.

OK, I shouldn't be happy.

I looked at another: "Don't let anyone tell you not
to celebrate in this moment. This is the justice we have
been waiting for."

Oh, OK, so I can be happy?

And another:

"This is not justice, this is accountability. They are
not the same."

*OK, that sounds good—maybe I'll just repost that because I
have to say something right now.*

I did this for a while, and I reposted and deleted a
few things, until finally I just closed the app, looked at
my wife, and said, "I actually just feel like I want to cry."
So I sat on the couch and cried with my wife.

In that moment, I was more concerned with presenting a version of myself that would keep my connection to a group strong, and I was severely disconnected from what I was actually feeling.

Can you relate to this?

Recall a time you tailored the way you said something on social media for fear of the response. How did you alter your words?

....

....

....

....

....

....

....

....

What have you posted online to stay in good standing with your selected group?

....

....

....

....

....

....

....

Recall a time when you posted something with absolutely no fact-checking because everyone in your chosen internet community was sharing it. Why did you choose to make that post?

....

....

....

....

....

....

....

....

There's a scene in *Mean Girls* that describes Cady Heron's new cult-like following after becoming friends with the most popular mean girls in school. A student recounts, "I saw Cady Heron wearing army pants and flip-flops, so I bought army pants and flip-flops."

That's how the internet feels sometimes: "This influencer posted it, so I posted it."

I think we all know what it's like to have a curated version of ourselves. That used to be an experience unique to celebrities and public figures, but now we all have these disparate parts of ourselves that we must piece together to keep our loose connections to a version of community only found on the internet.

What part or parts of your life would you never share on social media?

....
....
....
....
....
....
....
....

What is something you do that, if you shared it online, would get you critiqued?

....
....
....
....
....
....
....
....
....

I think that sometimes the opposite is true as well and that we use the internet as the place where we get to show up as the people that we want to be in our real lives.

My fear is that we are able to be radical on X (Twitter) and silent at the dinner table.

Have you ever posted something on the internet that you would absolutely never say to someone in person? What was it?

....

....

....

....

....

....

....

....

....

....

Here is the tension: The internet is a two-dimensional, transactional space. Our real lived experiences are not. Now, I'm not saying the internet isn't real, but it certainly falls short of capturing the whole experience of our human reality.

In *Do You Still Talk to Grandma?* I use the example of maps. If you were to look at a two-dimensional map of the United States and I asked you to draw a line from New York to Los Angeles, it would just be one long straight line. But if we were to look at a topographical map, we would need to bend and curve; there would be

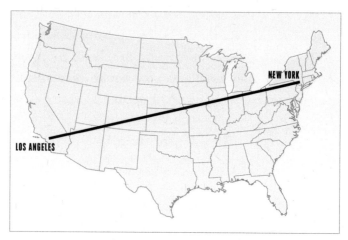

bridges to cross, mountains to curve around, high ground and low ground, and what once looked like a straight line is now a windy, curvy road.

The same is true for our experiences. If I asked you how you got to where you are now in your life, there's no way you just were born, went to school, got a job, got married, had kids, and now you're reading this book. Literally no one's life trajectory is that flat or straight. We have taken twists and turns and curves.

Here's what I want us to do. Below is an image of a river. The way rivers work is that they flow with gravity, but where they flow also can be changed by the big rocks that show up in their path. So if we think about our lives as a river, we can identify just a few of the rocks that have shaped our path.

I'll go first:

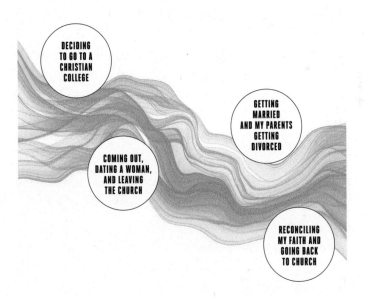

DECIDING TO GO TO A CHRISTIAN COLLEGE

GETTING MARRIED AND MY PARENTS GETTING DIVORCED

COMING OUT, DATING A WOMAN, AND LEAVING THE CHURCH

RECONCILING MY FAITH AND GOING BACK TO CHURCH

Now it's your turn:

Everyone's life looks like this. We have all experienced these rocks and curves, and our desire for community—real community—means traversing the curves together.

However, we are up against more than just our middle school selves wanting to fit in. Holding nuance and navigating the curves of community can be exhausting, and in times of intensity our brains can reject the seemingly endless web of nuance.

As you learned in *Do You Still Talk to Grandma?*, in 1989, the psychologist Arie Kruglanski coined the term "cognitive closure."

Cognitive closure is the point at which our brains decide that enough information has been gathered to make a decision.

Now, cognitive closure is a necessary part of our survival because, in a lot of ways, our lives are a never-ending series of decisions: when to wake up, what to eat for breakfast, what to wear to work, whom to date, where to go on a date, what breed of dog to get.

List ten decisions you have already made today:

....

....

....

....

....

....

....

....

....

....

You get it—we've got lots of decisions to make. So at some point, we need to stop taking in information and just . . . decide.

Cognitive closure is extremely helpful when you are doing something like crossing the street. Can you imagine if you never felt as if you had enough information to cross? You would be standing there for the rest of your life.

OK, let's break that down:

We have a function of our brains that allows us to stop taking in information and make decisions.

We take in all of the necessary information, and then we make a decision.

Standing on the street waiting to cross

↓

Looks both ways, sees no cars

↓

Crosses

OK, see how that works?

Pick one of the decisions you made today and let's do this again:

Where you started:

↓

....

....

....

The information you took in:

↓

....

....

....

The decision you made:

↓

....

....

....

It's simple, and it can be extremely helpful.

But our need for closure can also be extremely dangerous.

Our need for closure means that all of us have the potential to become extreme.

According to Arie Kruglanski, who has done extensive research in this area, the way we process information and make decisions changes dramatically in different circumstances, and during times of uncertainty, everyone's need for closure increases.

In times of uncertainty, our need for closure can trick our mind into thinking we already have the truth even though we haven't examined all of the evidence.

Remind you of anyone?

I am sure, right now as you are reading those words, you have a person, politician, social issue, or news channel in your mind that you feel is exploiting the human need for closure.

Who have you seen in our world that is exploiting the need for certainty and cognitive closure?

....

....

....

....

....

....

....

....

Who in your life has closed themselves off from accepting any new information and is certain they have the truth?

....

....

....

....

....

....

....

Have you ever tried to argue with this person (or these people)? How did it go?

....

....

....

....

....

....

....

Can you think of a time when you have been this person?

....

....

....

....

....

....

....

The notion that our brains, in times of uncertainty and fear, will latch on to the nearest idea that promises them certainty and security is very illuminating information for the current cultural climate we are in.

The reality is that to be a part of any extreme group, you have to close off your mind from accepting any new information. Makes sense, right?

Now, here's what gets really tricky about this: How do we know the difference between extremism and fighting for a just cause?

Can you define it? What is the difference between the extremism in the civil rights movement and the extremism of the insurrection on January 6, 2021?

Hopefully that was an easy one. But the murkiness of it comes when you step back and realize the same parts of our brains are activated when *we* get extreme, when we stop taking in new information—when we experience cognitive closure.

So what's the answer?

Let's keep digging.

Where are the places you are closed off to new information?

....
....
....
....
....
....

Where are the places you are feeling pressure to show up as the "most acceptable" version of yourself to stay connected to your community?

....
....
....
....
....
....
....

What nuance and information do you feel you have to find certainty about?

....
....
....
....
....
....

On a scale of 1 to 10, how much pressure do you feel to have ar-
rived at a place where you feel certain you have answers, and that
you are on the right side of the conversation? (Whatever the conver-
sation is: racism, homophobia, how to raise your kids, how to in-
vest money . . . you pick your current hot topic.)

No pressure at all									I NEED TO KNOW NOW
1	2	3	4	5	6	7	8	9	10

Our need for community, our tendency toward cognitive closure, and the presence of social media have all
fed off of one another in a way that has made everything seem urgent. We may not be able to fix this problem completely, but slowing down is a great place to
start.

3

Forgetting Progressive Amnesia

ALL RIGHT, IN CHAPTER 3 OF *DO YOU STILL TALK TO Grandma?*, I shared with you that Dave Chappelle and Kanye West used to be at the top of my hero list. I also shared the complications that have come since. Now it's your turn.

Who used to be at the top of your hero list that you feel embarrassed about now?

What are movies that you absolutely loved (and maybe still do) that don't hold up?

....
....
....
....
....
....
....

What is it about the movies that doesn't hold up?

....
....
....
....
....
....
....

As someone who has already shared with you both the joys and the pains of growing up evangelical, I can tell you a lot of things that I used to believe that I don't believe anymore. Some of them are far more painful than others.

I once had a Sunday school teacher tell me that there were video cameras recording every moment of my life, and that when I died, before I got into heaven, God would replay all of the tapes and decide if I could go in or not. OK, I meant to share that as one of the more silly things that I used to believe, but writing it out, I think that is actually kind of traumatizing—I will make a note to bring it up with my therapist.

But on to the more overtly painful things I have believed. I remember literally losing sleep at night wondering what was going to happen to me because I was gay. Would God hate me? Would bad things happen to me? I had adopted a belief that being gay was wrong, was a sin. That is absolutely one of the more painful things I have believed in my life.

The good news is that I no longer believe that there are cameras watching my every move (wow, was that Sunday school or Big Brother?) and I feel fully confident in my identity as a queer woman and a person of faith.

Before we go any further, it's your turn.

Write about something silly you used to believe that you no longer do:

....

....

....

....

....

....

....

....

Now write about something painful you used to believe, an ideology you subscribed to, or a narrative you bought into:

....

....

....

....

....

....

....

For me, there were so many conversations with friends, teachers, and mentors; so many books and movies; and so much therapy that helped me find myself on the other side of those harmful beliefs.

What are the things that helped you change your mind and believe something new?

....

....

....

....

....

....

....

....

....

How do you feel when you think back to the version of yourself that used to believe those things?

....

....

....

....

....

....

....

....

How do you feel about people who still believe in the ideas or narratives that you evolved out of?

....

....

....

....

....

....

....

....

I remember when I first started to deconstruct my faith, when I was at the very beginning of unraveling some of the harmful ideology and theology I had been handed. As soon as I was forced out of the community that believed those things, I started to think of everyone who was still there as beneath me. I saw myself as evolved and I saw them as, well, less evolved. They were antiquated, outdated, problematic, and yes, while all of that was true, they were also me six months prior to my own realizations.

Have you ever had an experience like that? When you learned something new, shed a harmful idea, and evolved in some way, how did it impact the way you saw the people who remained in the position you'd just left or evolved out of?

....

....

....

....

....

....

....

....

The line between "I just learned this" and "I can't believe everyone doesn't know this" is thin. And it's even thinner online.

The example I use in *Do You Still Talk to Grandma?* is one I think we have all encountered in some way or another online.

The exchange goes something like this. Our friend Lisa is wanting to cut back on dairy—her stomach has been acting funny and she thinks, "Hey, a little less milk couldn't hurt, right?" So Lisa goes to a coffee shop and orders a latte with almond milk for the first time. She's so excited about her new almond milk journey that she takes a cute picture of her latte and posts it online. Chaos ensues.

The first person to comment is another woman who, two hours prior, read an article about unfair coffee farming practices. She writes, "All the almond milk in the world can't cover the blood on your hands from drinking at Starbucks, Lisa."

Lisa, unaware of the article her internet friend stumbled upon earlier that morning, replies curiously, "Wait, what's wrong with Starbucks?"

Joining the comments is a new person who only five minutes ago heard that almond trees are causing a water shortage in California. They comment, "The problem is that while you're busy thinking about coffee farmers, your almond milk is killing the earth and soon there will be no planet to farm—did you ever think about that?!"

The first person replies, "Wow, so you're saying almonds are more important than human lives?"

A third person has an even hotter take: "Wow, both of you are completely missing the mark because it's not about the farmers or the almonds, it's capitalism, and if you can't see that, then I guess you're just another pawn in the capitalist scheme—and that actually makes me sad because I thought you were both smarter than that."

Finally, a fourth person reading along, this one a peripheral acquaintance of Lisa's, feels compelled to join in: "Hey, Lisa, so sorry to see that you're not a conscious consumer of coffee or almonds. I'd hoped we could build a friendship, but after reading these comments and seeing your lack of response here, it makes me wonder if you're even the type of person I want to follow on here. I'm gonna go, and I hope you find the resources to educate yourself about what's really important."

Lisa is now in tears, not drinking her latte.

Did that exchange feel familiar?

Write about an exchange you've seen or been a part of online that felt similar:

....

....

....

....

....

....

....

....

....

Think of the times you witnessed progressive amnesia (someone conveniently forgetting about the time before they came to know what they know now), and list them in the following areas:

POLITICALLY   **SOCIALLY**   **PERSONALLY**

....

....

....

....

....

....

....

....

Why do you think we do this? Why do you think it feels easy to demonize someone for standing where we stood moments before?

....

....

....

....

....

....

....

....

I think often about my exit from church. I try to stay close to the memory of what it felt like to be six months outside that community, and how I immediately felt as if I were better than everyone else who was still in the community. They were pre-evolved and antiquated, and I was moving forward, growing, healing.

Sure, some of that is true—harmful ideology in that space had caused me pain, and I felt more freedom in my life after I left.

But what was it that allowed me to almost immediately feel better than the people who were still in that building? Were they antiquated prehistoric idiots—or were they just me six months ago?

I definitely think it's both/and. We can be proud of our progress, we can stand against the oppressive and harmful ideologies in our world, and we can also hold empathy for the people who are stuck in the same places we have escaped from.

To resist progressive amnesia, understand that you are on a spiral staircase, and as you go up, don't forget to look down once in a while and view your past from a new vantage point. We need to hold on to a sense of complexity, about ourselves and others, if we ever hope to get past progressive amnesia and move forward together.

4

Whatever You Do, Don't Get Canceled

THE TERM *CANCELED* WAS NOT ALWAYS IN POPULAR
culture or found in everyday conversation, but in
my relatively short lifetime, I have witnessed all
sorts of "cancellations." I grew up in the nineties, and
I very clearly remember all of the details surrounding
the scandal involving our then president, Bill Clinton.
Do you remember that time? This scandal was all
anyone could talk about, and in just about every news
segment on every channel, every talk show, every magazine, it seemed as if the same questions were being
asked.

Could we still let this person be our president after
he'd disappointed us? Was this personal moral failure
severe enough to end his professional successes? Could
we ever trust him again? Could he ever come back from

this? What would be an appropriate consequence for his actions?

We were all—across the country and even across the world—trying to wrap our minds around how to deal with a powerful public figure who had just shat the bed in a big way. The conversation about Clinton's affair with White House intern Monica Lewinsky affected every corner of thought and information. Did it matter that he was in a position of power and much older? That he was her boss? Were we, as the public, owed the details of the president's sex life? It was all confusing, it was all complicated, and it was fascinating, as a pre-teen, to witness these conversations happening on the news, at school, in living rooms across the country. I certainly heard them from my parents and their friends. These questions even made their way to the fifth-grade lunch tables.

What to do with someone in a public position who'd just had a big public failure? My friends and I would ask one another: Do you think the president is gonna be fired? Would you vote for him? I had a personal affinity for President Clinton because he appeared in the opening theme song of my absolute favorite cartoon, *Animaniacs*. So no, my decision-making skills were not yet fully developed or trustworthy.

What is the first public scandal you remember? What were the questions that surrounded it?

....

....

....

....

....

....

....

These questions aren't new. I've been asking them since the fifth grade with my friends, and I am sure many people were asking them long before that. Our disappointments with public figures are not new either. So what is different about the time we find ourselves in now?

There are a few big changes we have experienced culturally—and perhaps the biggest is the fact that we have all become public figures. A whole lot of us have decided that our personal opinions on public figures need to be shared, and we are living in a social environment we all know as *cancel culture.*

This has become such common language that even Dictionary.com, in its Pop Culture Dictionary, has a definition for us:

> *Cancel culture* refers to the popular practice of withdrawing support for (*canceling*) public figures and companies after they have done or said something considered objectionable or offensive. *Cancel culture* is generally discussed as being

performed on social media in the form of group shaming.

Our new experience of all being public figures with public voices has created the situation we find ourselves in.

OK, now I want you to think of a more recent celebrity scandal. Got it? What was different between the first example you gave and this more recent one?

....

....

....

....

....

....

....

Did the celebrity in your recent example get canceled? What did that look like?

....

....

....

....

....

....

....

....

Did you participate in any way? What was your participation?

....

....

....

....

....

....

....

....

....

....

Most of us, at this point, know the anatomy of a celebrity cancellation or what it looks like when a celebrity performs the necessary steps to avoid cancellation.

This is how it goes:

1. A person does something *wrong*.
2. An internet mob comes after them.
3. The person starts losing business.
4. They post a public apology video.
5. They lie low for a minute.
6. They come back.

Pick a celebrity, pick a scandal, and I'm sure they ticked all those boxes.

I remember when Ellen DeGeneres got canceled

for a moment recently, and when people were mad at Blake Lively and Ryan Reynolds because they got married at a plantation. I remember when the Dixie Chicks changed their name to just "The Chicks," to avoid associations with the Confederacy and Southern slavery.

It's great; I love that people are realizing that a plantation is an absolutely insane place to get married, or that maybe you shouldn't be named Dixie anything . . . and I can't remember what Ellen was accused of—I think it was something related to how she treated her employees—but I'm sure she learned something helpful too.

Now listen, I know there is a huge difference between Ellen and Harvey Weinstein. Just so you know, when we refer to cancel culture in this context, we are not talking about crimes. We are talking about what to do with people whose ignorance, bias, sexism, racism, homophobia, and so on shows up. How do we respond, and is what we are doing right now working?

In *Do You Still Talk to Grandma?* I reference an article from *New York* magazine, "Canceled at 17." It seemed as though it could be a big step toward having a broader conversation, but shortly after the story was published, the backlash came swiftly.

But before we get into that, let's ask ourselves some questions that are going to require you to get in touch with your teenage self.

Can you remember anyone in your high school who was ostracized? Why was that person on the outside of whatever community you had?

....

....

....

....

....

....

....

In what ways did you passively participate in keeping that person out of your community? (For example, "I sat at the same lunch table every day, and we never invited anyone new.")

....

....

....

....

....

....

....

....

In what ways did you actively participate in keeping that person out of your community? (For example, "I spread rumors" or "I chose not to invite the person to an event I organized.")

....

....

Describe a time you were bullied, or a time when you acted as a bully.

Let's talk about these present realities now . . .

Have you ever participated in someone's cancellation on social media? What did it look like? A share? A comment? A repost?

Have you ever told a person in their comments how much they have disappointed you? Or given them additional critique for a mistake they were sharing? What did it feel like?

....

....

....

....

....

....

I think we have all heard the term *Karen.* Do you remember when you first heard it? It has definitely gone from a novel thing to part of our everyday vernacular.

How would you describe what a Karen is to someone who had no idea?

....

....

....

....

....

....

....

....

A few months ago I was on a plane, and a man and a woman, two fully grown adults, in the row ahead of me got into a big, loud argument. They were both on aisle seats of the same row. They were strangers when they boarded this plane, and I feel confident saying they were enemies by the time we landed and deplaned. But the most interesting part of their argument was when the man, so fed up, just said, "I don't argue with Karens," and the women said, "Is that supposed to be an insult? I love being a Karen."

So let's talk about Karens . . .

Referring to people as Karens has become common language in most parts of our culture, and what started as a term to describe middle-aged white women who ask to speak to the manager, or who call the police on a Black man who is bird-watching, has since expanded to include anyone who seems hell-bent on making sure everyone obeys the rules. And what are the rules, you ask? Well, the rules are different for every Karen, but they all believe in them with the same vigor.

Have you ever had an interaction with a Karen? What was it like?

....

....

....

....

....

....

Karens are the people on the internet—and in real life—who take it upon themselves to right every "wrong," and to address any and all behavior they deem a mistake or misstep.

Are Karens the new trolls?

But why do they exist? How did we get here?

Well, I think there are lots of complicated Karen layers to unpack. We've got privilege and power colliding with responsibility, all being held together by what I like to call superhero syndrome.

Here are three things I think are true about Karens:

1. They have some sort of privilege.
2. They only see the world around them, not themselves.
3. They think they are doing something right.

OK, let's break this down—let's use a real Karen example.

I don't know why, but since the start of the Covid pandemic and with the rise of TikTok, there has been a lot more conversation about dogs. What to feed your dog, the right way to train your dog, how much enrichment your dog should have. Let me assure you right now, if you thought you were doing a good job with your dog, you're not doing well enough.

Now, as a person who actually makes her own dog

food because we have the best pup with the most sensitive stomach, I thought I was doing a good job until I saw some of these videos. But that's beside the point.

There is a woman I follow who happened to post a video of herself in her kitchen, and there in the background was the dog food. It was kibble—the food that most of the dogs in our society eat. But a woman in the comment section became absolutely irate.

"How could you feed your dog kibble? You wouldn't eat McDonald's every day, would you?"

"It is obvious you don't care about your dog. He needs to be taken away from you."

"I hope you don't treat your kids like you treat your dog."

The comments were becoming more and more unhinged. Then the woman started commenting on every other comment from this video with the words:

"Please don't follow this person, she is a murderer."

That's intense! But it's not uncommon.

I think we have all seen the Karens of the internet who continually and habitually take things this far.

Let's look at those three Karen truths again:

1. They have some sort of privilege.
2. They only see the world around them, not themselves.
3. They think they are doing something right.

1. They have some sort of privilege.

What privileges might you assume about the woman making the comments about dog kibble?

....

....

....

....

....

....

....

....

2. They see only the world around them, not themselves.

Why do you think Karens are so drawn to focusing almost exclusively on others and not themselves?

....

....

....

....

....

....

....

....

3. They think they are doing something right.

What was the "right thing" this woman might have thought she was doing?

....

....

....

....

....

....

....

OK, we definitely have a problem with Karens on the internet. They might be the extreme versions, but all of us share some of the same qualities.

What privileges do you have in your life?

....

....

....

....

....

....

....

....

....

Describe a time in your life when you were angry or stressed or disappointed, but, instead of addressing the issue, you just passed it on to someone else.

....

....

....

....

....

....

....

....

Describe an instance when you thought you were doing something right or good but, you now realize, you were actually doing something harmful.

....

....

....

....

....

....

....

....

The anatomy of a Karen lives in all of us, and it is going to take a commitment to self-awareness and growth to keep us from lying in our room at one in the morning, phone in hand, calling someone a murderer for feeding their dog kibble.

But Karens are a crucial part of the cancel culture we live in. They are one of the reasons we have stretched and pulled the consequences of certain actions as far as they can go.

Before we talk about consequences and punishments, I've got a couple questions for you.

Do you think canceling people should happen? Why or why not?

....

....

....

....

....

....

....

What would you change about cancel culture?

....

....

....

....

....

....

....

5

The Lost Art of Making Mistakes

FOR THIS NEXT SECTION, I AM GOING TO INVITE YOU TO think of a mistake that you have made. For most of us living, breathing human beings, this should not take very long.

Got it? Now that you have the mistake in your mind, let's answer a few questions about it. But you need to really make sure you can put yourself right back in the moment of remembering what it felt like.

In *Do You Still Talk to Grandma?* I share the story of the time I forgot to push the record button and someone's entire wedding ceremony went unfilmed. Truly, even writing about that moment, I was reminded of everything, from the way my face felt as it went ghost white, to the pit in my stomach, to the guilt I had as I listened to my wife call and tell the couple what happened. That was six years ago, and I still remember how it felt.

Let's see what you remember.

The mistake:

....

....

....

....

....

....

How did it feel physically?

....

....

....

....

....

....

How did it feel emotionally?

....

....

....

....

....

....

....

....

What impact did it have on your personal relations?

....

....

....

....

....

....

What (if any) were the consequences?

....

....

....

....

....

....

How do you feel thinking about it now?

....

....

....

....

....

Now that we are remembering what it feels like to make a mistake, let's see if we can also identify what it feels like to be on the receiving end of a mistake.

Back when I was dating men, my college boyfriend cheated on me with my roommate. (Scandalous, right?)

Although he was definitely not the person I wanted to end up with, his mistake still impacted me, and I can remember how it felt physically finding that out. I remember how it felt emotionally. It obviously impacted multiple levels of my life relationally, and if I am honest, I feel as though the consequences on his end were minimal. But now, fifteen or so years later when I think about that mistake I was on the receiving end of, it truly doesn't bother me.

But what about you? Let's take a look at the receiving end of a mistake.

The mistake:

How did it feel physically?

....

....

....

....

....

....

....

How did it feel emotionally?

....

....

....

....

....

....

What impact did it have on your personal relations?

....

....

....

....

....

....

What (if any) were the consequences?

....

....

....

....

....

....

....

How do you feel thinking about it now?

....

....

....

....

....

....

We all know that mistakes are measured on a sliding scale. There is a big difference between falling down when you are learning how to ride a bike and cheating on a partner. All mistakes are not created equally.

Let's take a look at some different types of mistakes.

The Dennis Learning Center at Ohio State University has researched and identified four types of mistakes: stretch mistakes, a-ha moment mistakes, sloppy mistakes, and high-stakes mistakes.

TYPE OF MISTAKE: STRETCH MISTAKE
Definition
Instructive mistakes made by trying to do something that is beyond what we have previously been able to do successfully
My Example
Learning a new language and confusing *thank you* with *Where's the bathroom?*
Your Example

TYPE OF MISTAKE: A-HA MOMENT MISTAKE
Definition
Instructive mistakes in which we realize that what we've done was not effective
My Example
Finding a shortcut to work and realizing you could shave an extra five minutes off your drive time
Your Example

TYPE OF MISTAKE: SLOPPY MISTAKE
Definition
Mistakes made by losing focus while doing something that we know well
My Example
Poking your eye trying to put mascara on in a hurry
Your Example

TYPE OF MISTAKE: HIGH-STAKES MISTAKE
Definition
Mistakes made by taking risks in high-stakes situations
My Example
Letting your own insecurities take over and self-sabotaging a relationship
Your Example

No, all mistakes are not created equal, but mistakes are inevitable.

When you are doing life with other human beings, mistakes will happen because of you, and you will witness mistakes around you, and some of those mistakes will feel as if they are being done to you.

Since we cannot avoid mistakes, the best we can do is get better at learning from them. And the number one rule of learning from mistakes is simple: Go slow.

Neuroscientists at NYU have found that our brains are wired to move more slowly and to take more time after a mistake, which makes sense. If you cut your finger chopping garlic, you are likely going to chop a lot more carefully the next time that knife is in your hand.

You get it. After a mistake, your brain needs time to slow down, pay more attention, and create new pathways. You poke your eye with mascara—you put it on more slowly next time. You leave your coffee on top of the car and drive away, and you'll open the door and put it in the cup holder next time. But a lot of us have a harder time when it comes to emotional and relational mistakes.

I don't know many people who cut their finger chopping garlic, and instead of slowing down, creating more efficient and productive chopping habits, they just said, "I'm done cooking forever."

To move on from a mistake, a person has to be open

and mature enough to say, "Maybe I wasn't appropriately using the knife, maybe I was distracted, I bet I can find a way to do this again safely."

But when we get hurt relationally or emotionally, or we find ourselves getting hurt in a situation that we can just avoid, we often think it's easier to give up altogether than to do all of the relational work necessary to slow down, rewire, and repair our relationships safely with other mistake-ridden human beings. Sometimes it truly isn't safe enough to continue in a relationship with a person who has wronged you, but forgiveness is still possible, and there is still relational work to be done around the situation you were in with them.

Forgiveness is sticky and messy, and it can feel like a moving target. But let's see if we can find some places that have hit our lives in a real, tangible way.

Who in your life do you feel you have forgiven?

What are the signs that you have forgiven them?

....

....

....

....

....

....

....

Who in your life are you still working on forgiving? What do you feel are the barriers in that process?

....

....

....

....

....

....

....

Who in your life are you waiting for forgiveness from? How might that forgiveness impact you?

....

....

....

....

This work is complicated. It requires us to be able to hold multiple truths at the same time. We are healing from mistakes and wounds that people have given to us, and we are exercising the maturity that it takes to heal and move on from the mistakes that we have made and the wounds we have caused.

If you think you land fully on one side of that line, you are mistaken (pun intended).

Not making mistakes is not an option. It takes maturity to make mistakes well. It takes slow forgiveness to heal from the mistakes others have made. These two realities dance together in what I believe is our best bet at moving forward.

If I asked you to make a list of every mistake you have ever made, we would run out of paper.

If I got more specific and asked you to make a list of every ignorant thing you have ever said, well, we would probably still run out of paper. But what if I asked you to make a list of all of the consequences that resulted from your ignorant statements?

The racist joke you told in middle school? The antiquated ideas you wrote papers about in college? Your uninformed voting record?

The goal isn't to create a world where everyone is born knowing everything they need to know in order to never make a mistake—that's not even realistic. But I think the issue that we are presently faced with, given that nobody is born with an informed political consciousness, and that nobody has inherited infinite knowledge, is this: What do we do when those jokes are made? What do we do when the votes are cast and the papers are written?

Are we creating consequences that allow for maturity, slowing down, and creating new neural pathways, or are we creating punishments that breed shame and speedy apologies?

6

Accountability, Not Annihilation

HAVE YOU EVER THOUGHT ABOUT THE DIFFERENCE BE-
tween consequences and punishments? To be completely honest, it wasn't until I'd started researching
for this book that I had thought about it in such detail.
I always intuitively knew there was a difference—I think
we all do. I think we can all see the difference between
what happens when a teenager misses curfew so they
aren't allowed to go out the next weekend versus a teenager who misses curfew so the door gets taken off their
room and they have to wear a shirt to school that says
"I don't know how to tell time." There is a difference
between consequences and punishments, and it is important that we know that difference.

Consequences are meant to teach, maintain accountability, and maintain safety. But the goal of a punishment is to shame, guilt, assert authority, or harm.

All right, let's see if we've got this. I am going to give you a scenario, and you come up with some consequences and punishments to make sure we understand the difference.

Scenario: You have a seven-year-old kid who was playing baseball in the house (something they are not allowed to do), and they break a window.

CONSEQUENCE	PUNISHMENT

Now that we are thinking through the consequences-versus-punishments lens, let's go back to the mistakes that we were thinking about in chapter 5.

Recall a time when you experienced a consequence for a mistake.

How did it feel?

Recall a time when you were punished for a mistake.

....

....

....

How did it feel?

....

....

....

....

....

....

....

Now, because we are self-aware and self-reflective folks . . .

Recall a time you imposed consequences on someone for their mistake.

....

....

....

....

....

....

....

....

Recall a time when you punished someone.

....

....

....

....

....

....

....

My journey into understanding the difference between consequences and punishments led me down a "gentle parenting" rabbit hole. If you are over the age of thirty, gentle parenting is probably not how you were raised, but if you have kids now, I am sure you have heard about it. I don't have or want kids, and even I've heard about it.

This parenting style is composed of four main elements—empathy, respect, understanding, and boundaries. Gentle parenting focuses on fostering the qualities you want in your child by being compassionate while also enforcing consistent boundaries. In other words, gentle parenting is all about consequences—never punishments.

The four elements of gentle parenting can help us understand the broader anatomy of consequences.

Think of the last celebrity or public figure you saw or heard about making a mistake. What happened to them? Did they experience consequences or punishments? Was it a mixture of both?

One of the difficult things about being an adult in the real world is that there are no more parents. If our favorite celebrity uses a word they aren't supposed to use, or tweets something they aren't supposed to tweet, or steps out of line in any way—who determines the consequences? Who creates the punishments?

Let's see if we can use the gentle parenting elements to think through what some appropriate celebrity consequences might be.

Let's start with a real-life example. Have you ever been at a family holiday gathering where you hear a distant relative or grandparent say something that would absolutely get a celebrity canceled on social media? I am guessing that what happens with someone like a grandparent is this:

EMPATHY

I have a lot of empathy for Grandma, for the fact that up until a few years ago absolutely no one told her that some of the things she believed were wrong, and I am sure she feels scared and attacked, and that's not something that I would want to feel. I can have empathy for the fact that she has lived her life one way unchecked and the rules have now changed.

RESPECT

Grandma? I do respect her, love her, and can appreciate the ways she has been here, and ultimately the fact that she has done what she needed to do to survive. Does she understand queer theory? Absolutely not. Do I think I would have survived her particular circumstances? Also no.

UNDERSTANDING

To be honest, I can understand how fast the world has moved, and I know why my Grandma had a look of horror on her face when she heard me say the word *queer*. I explained that the word is OK now and we like it. But the world she grew up in was different, and the world around her is changing at a rapid pace. So Grandma? No, I don't agree with her, but I can have empathy for the very large ground the world has asked her to cover in a short time.

BOUNDARIES

Now, just because I can have empathy and understanding for why Grandma is the way she is and says what she says, that does not mean that I don't have boundaries. Maybe I feel differently about them, maybe I even grieve the boundaries, but Grandma is out of line, is not creating a safe environment, and that will have consequences. We hope those consequences and boundaries come as a result of empathy, respect, and understanding. That's how we get to consequences and not punishments. That's how we set boundaries with Grandma instead of making a Facebook group called "someone come get my grandma."

Your turn. Think of the person in your life who has made the type of mistake that would absolutely get them canceled if they were a celebrity, and walk through these four elements:

EMPATHY

RESPECT

UNDERSTANDING

BOUNDARIES

A few years ago, I saw a video of Justin Bieber sing-
ing the N-word. I know, right? It was an old video that
had resurfaced for some reason or another, and people
on the internet were outraged—calling for an apology,
for brands to drop him, for his tour to get canceled.

I gave in to temptation and finally went and watched
the video. It's not the type of video I am usually eager to
click on or watch, but I was curious. I know, I have seen
videos of a hundred white celebrities letting this word
slip out of their mouths not knowing they were on camera, and then they cry through an apology—it's the way
it goes. But this video was different. It was sad to me in
a different way. Justin was fourteen years old when the
video was shot, but he looks even younger, like a child.
He is sitting on a chair in front of a backdrop—he has
obviously just done an interview or is preparing for
one. The very nice and, I am sure, very big camera is
pointed right at him, and this little boy sings the words
to his song "One Less Lonely Girl," only he replaces
the word *girl* with the N-word. It is so awful and cringey.
It's even worse because he sings the line not once but
several times.

Now, here is what I found even more infuriating.
The camera is pointed only at Justin, but because he is
a child, and also because of how many people it takes to
make a set run, I know for a fact there are many adults
in that room. As Justin initially, sheepishly sings the lyric
the first time, you watch as his eyes scan the room—

knowing this may not be something he is supposed to do. He looks around at all the adults with eyes asking, "Is this OK?" And you hear absolutely nothing—until one faint chuckle in the background. And so he does it again.

I am not saying that Justin Bieber does not deserve consequences for using a word that he knew was not supposed to be used, but I would be out of my mind if I couldn't find some empathy and understanding for a fourteen-year-old kid in a room full of adults ready to let him do absolutely anything he wanted because their paychecks depended on him. It was a tragic thing to watch.

Yes. Actions demand and require consequences.

No, shame and punishments do not work.

Having empathy, respect, and understanding does not keep us from setting boundaries and determining consequences, but hopefully it can keep us from shame and punishment.

I will never forget when my friend Rachel Hollis was going through her own cancellation. She had posted a video that was absolutely out of line and that put a bright focus on her own blind spots. Her ties to white supremacy as a wealthy white woman in her thirties had become front and center, and she experienced the consequences for making that video.

As her friend, it was easy for me to hold those four elements—empathy, respect, understanding, and boundaries. This video she made did not erase the years of friendship and relationship we had, but it was also hurtful. I held it all together at the same time and then decided what my appropriate boundaries and consequences would be. But what I was reading in her comment sections was something else entirely.

For context, this incident happened not long after Rachel's ex-husband had just gone public with a new relationship, and the number of comments I read that went something like "Your ex's new girlfriend is prettier than you" was astonishing.

Why do we do that? Why do we want punishments so badly? Why do consequences not feel like enough?

Rachel lost a brand deal with Target, got dropped from speaking engagements, was forced to cancel tours, and had some very direct conversations with the people in her life whom she had disappointed. Relationships and professional opportunities were lost, and the trajectory of her career shifted. I am not saying this so that you feel bad for her. These were the consequences that came with her actions. So why did so many people need to add shame on top of that?

Have you ever noticed the sort of frenzy that happens when someone is pulled into the proverbial town square? It feels as though whatever actions or crimes they have committed become an opportunity to throw all of the stones that we have been collecting our whole lives, and instead of asking about appropriate consequences, we start a shouting match that amounts to "I am hurting, so I want you to hurt, too."

Let's be honest: A lot of times we don't want consequences, we don't want accountability, we want shame—we want annihilation.

That quest to be the bringers of annihilation has caused us to do some interesting things.

The dissenting voice has always been an important part of dialogue and education. It took a couple of brave souls to argue that the world is round, and their dissent gave us the knowledge we have today (well, except for the people who still believe it's flat, but that's another issue).

But now we have turned the dissenting voice into a never-ending search for what is wrong.

At the beginning of pandemic times and the "oh no, everyone just found out America is racist" times, there were a lot of materials being shared, and a lot of them had titles like "Ten Things to Do If . . ." or "Ten Ways to Start Your Antiracism Journey" or "Fifteen Things You Can Say to Your Racist Boss."

Then at some point, there was a shift. Instead of those articles and blog posts leading the way, the content I was seeing on everyone's pages turned to "Ten Things Wrong with Your Antiracism Books" or "Three Ways These Popular Activists Missed the Mark" or "Five Ways to Tell Your Friends Are Fake Activists." We went from sharing information to creating entire platforms based on poking holes in other people's ideas. Not creating content—critiquing content. Don't get me wrong, I think critique is extremely important, but when the majority of content shifts from construction to deconstruction, I think we've got a problem.

Do you remember the article that I mentioned earlier, "Canceled at 17"? Well, that article caught massive amounts of critique almost immediately after publication. Someone was critiquing the culture of critique? Everyone had something to say about it.

The article chronicled the experience of a high school student who had been effectively "canceled" by classmates. Ostracized, shunned, shamed. You get it. Well, the article did a great job of highlighting that all of this came as the result of an actual mistake the student had made. He got drunk at a party and showed a nude photo of his girlfriend to a few friends. That is bad, that deserves consequences—but what he received was punishment.

One of the main critiques I read about the article (and I read a lot) was that it was wrong to center the story on the person who did something wrong. People were mad that this kid's "side of the story" was being shared. That critique for me just further highlighted our issues: When it's not us or someone we love, we allow people who make mistakes to become "other" and "less than." We advance the punishment and annihilation narratives. We throw a fit because an article was written about a high school student facing annihilation over accountability. We throw empathy out the door if we see an opportunity to critique.

When the need to be right outweighs our desire to be human, we will always seek punishment over consequences.

7

Boundaries to the Rescue

S O WHAT DO WE DO WITH REPEAT OFFENDERS? WHAT do we do when the people around us do not allow their mistakes to be teachers? What do we do when we do not have the emotional resources to be gentle, or to access empathy and understanding?

Well, the simple answer is that we just honor where we are and set boundaries appropriately. Yes, in an ideal world we are always able to access our empathy and understanding, and in that same ideal world, the people around us use their mistakes as guides to growth and change.

But in the real world, that is not always the case.

I remember listening to a podcast with a gentle parenting expert, and she raved about gentle parenting and all of the amazing things that it can do in the world and for the lives of her children, and how much time she has spent studying and researching. Then she said, "Just for context, I am successfully gently parenting about one fourth of the time."

Yes, these may be our goals or the mindsets and strategies that we believe in, but we will not be able to accomplish them one hundred percent of the time.

To better understand this concept, I want us to take a close look at the racial identity development model created by Dr. Derald Wing Sue and Dr. David Sue. This particular model was taught to me in college, and it not only gave me many insights into my own identity development but it also taught me one of the most important lessons about identity I have ever learned.

There are two models, one for BIPOC folks and one for white folks, because each have different experiences in the world. We are going to go through each model and talk about what it means for us.

For each stage, I will give you the definition and an example of what it can look like in our lives, and then I am going to invite you to come up with an example from your own life. If there is any stage that you feel you have never experienced, it's OK to skip that one. This model is meant to help us understand a broader framework; it is not a test.

First up, the model for BIPOC folks:

STAGE: CONFORMITY

Definition

In this stage, you experience a positive attitude toward and even a preference for dominant (white) cultural values. You place considerable value on characteristics that represent the dominant cultural group. You may even devalue or hold negative views of your own race or other racial/ethnic groups that are not part of the dominant white culture.

My Example

In my conformity stage, I placed considerable value on European beauty standards, and specifically I saw perfectly straight hair as something to aspire to. Not because I preferred the style, but because I thought it was a more appropriate and acceptable way to wear my hair.

Your Example

STAGE: DISSONANCE AND APPRECIATING

Definition

In this stage, you begin to question identity. You start to recognize conflicting messages or observe problems that challenge the beliefs and stereotypes about your own cultural group. You may also begin to question the value you have put on mainstream (white) cultural groups. You develop a growing sense of your own cultural heritage as well as a growing awareness of the existence of racism. You also move away from seeing dominant cultural groups as all good.

My Example

This experience started in a significant way for me in high school when I was first introduced to *The Autobiography of Malcolm X*. In reading that book, I was forced not only to deal with the presence of racism but also to recognize and question the value that I had placed on white culture, oftentimes placing it above my own.

Your Example

RESISTANCE AND IMMERSION

This stage is where you embrace and hold a positive attitude toward and preference for your own race. In this stage, you will reject dominant values of society and culture. You begin to focus on eliminating oppression within your own racial/cultural group. You will most likely experience big feelings, including distrust and anger toward dominant cultural groups and anything that may represent them. You place considerable value on characteristics that represent your own cultural group without question. You also likely develop a growing appreciation for others from racially and culturally diverse groups.

My Example

This was me after reading *The Autobiography of Malcolm X*, which led me down a rabbit hole of all sorts of Black authors and leaders whom I had never heard of. I became obsessed with only reading Black authors, and I became extremely aware of racism and all of its evils. I developed lots of anger toward the white culture that surrounded me. And in my reading of all of these Black authors, I was also led to learn about Latinx revolutionaries and AAPI heroes I had never heard of. In this stage, I swung from wanting to have straight hair to being anti-white. It felt like us versus them every day.

Your Example

STAGE: INTROSPECTION

Definition

In the introspection stage, you begin to question the psychological cost of projecting strong feelings toward dominant (white) cultural groups. You desire to refocus more energy on your own personal identity while respecting your own cultural groups. You begin to realign perspective to note that not all aspects of white dominant cultural groups, and not all aspects of your own racial/cultural group or other diverse groups, are wholly good or bad. You might experience and struggle with a conflict of loyalty as the binary breaks down and your perspective broadens.

My Example

It is hard to be angry all the time. This is the stage where I started to open up and allow myself to take a closer look—to see if any groups were all bad or all good, to start to be open to new voices, to allow more than one thing to be true. Yes, I hate racism, and no, I don't have to hate all white people.

Your Example

STAGE: INTEGRATIVE AWARENESS

Definition

In this stage, you have developed a secure, confident sense of your own racial/cultural identity and you become multi-cultural. You maintain pride in your own racial identity, you commit to supporting and appreciating all oppressed and diverse groups, and you tend to recognize racism as a societal illness by which all can be victimized.

My Example

This is the stage that I am in when I can see that the system of racism has impacted everyone. I will continue to fight for all oppressed and marginalized groups while allowing myself to hold true to the dignity of every human being. I have been here a time or two in my life, perhaps when I am my most integrated self and there is nothing stressful or upsetting happening in the world, but this is definitely not a realistic place to be one hundred percent of the time.

Your Example

Next, let's take a look at the model for our white friends.

STAGE: NAÏVETÉ

Definition

In this stage, you have an early childhood developmental phase of curiosity or minimal awareness of race. You may not receive any specific and overt messages about other racial/cultural groups, but overall you possess a white ethnocentric view of culture.

My Example

In this stage for white folks, race truly is not thought about or talked about. You have a preference for whiteness and view the world through a white lens, but you don't know that yet. This was everyone in 2020 who made a comment like "I have never thought about any of this before," and it was a factually true statement.

Your Example

STAGE: CONFORMITY

Definition

In the conformity stage, you have minimal awareness of yourself as a racial person. You believe strongly in the universality of values and norms. You perceive white American cultural groups as more highly developed, and you may justify the disparity of treatment other groups receive. You may be unaware of beliefs that reflect this—the message is so ingrained in you that you don't realize it's not universal.

My Example

This is the stage that folks are in when they make statements like "We are all just American." Yes, you may have become aware of race, but you are still moving the focus off of race and toward conforming to cultural norms. Those cultural norms are rooted in whiteness, but you may not be aware of that.

Your Example

STAGE: DISSONANCE

Definition

The dissonance stage is when you begin to experience an opportunity to examine your own prejudices and biases. You move toward the realization that dominant white society oppresses racially and culturally diverse groups. You may begin to feel shame, anger, and depression about the perpetuation of racism by white American culture, and you might begin to question previously held beliefs.

My Example

This is the stage I would say that a lot of white people in our country fell into in 2020. After your eyes are opened and you move past conformity, you are going to feel dissonance. I saw this in my white friends who would consistently say that they felt bad about being white.

Your Example

STAGE: RESISTANCE AND IMMERSION

Definition

In this stage, you have increased awareness of your own racism and how racism is projected in society, for example through media and language. You likely feel angry about messages concerning other racial and cultural groups and guilty for being part of an oppressive system. You might counteract these feelings by assuming a paternalistic role and thinking you know what is best for other groups without their involvement. You can also experience overidentifying with another racial/cultural group.

My Example

This is when the development becomes personal, and instead of just feeling sad about racism, you become aware of the ways that you have personally participated, and you become eager to show something else. An example of this would be a white person who feels bad about their role in the racist education system, so they start a nonprofit to help students of color.

Your Example

STAGE: INTROSPECTION

Definition

Introspection causes you to begin to redefine what it means to be a white American and to be a racial and cultural being. You begin to recognize the inability to fully understand the experience of others from diverse racial and cultural backgrounds, and you may feel disconnected from the white American group.

My Example

This is the stage where you begin to reconcile what it means to be white and also where you stop trying to align yourself with or fully understand people of color and focus more on your own identity and understanding. This is the stage where folks might pick up the book *White Fragility,* or where they stop apologizing to their Black friends and instead initiate conversations about privilege and white identity with their white friends.

Your Example

STAGE: INTEGRATIVE AWARENESS

Definition

This stage allows you to appreciate racial, ethnic, and cultural diversity. You understand yourself as a racial and cultural being. You become aware of sociopolitical influences of racism, and you begin to internalize a nonracist identity.

My Example

As you learn more, you begin asking, "What does this look like for me?" In this stage, you are more tied to your own identity, are aware of the presence of racism, and want to appreciate other groups all at the same time. This could look like continuing your own education through books or podcasts, expanding the art and information you consume to come from diverse sources, and continuing on your self-awareness journey.

Your Example

STAGE: COMMITMENT TO ANTIRACIST ACTION

Definition

In this stage, you commit to social action to eliminate oppression and racist disparity. You are likely to feel pressure from your dominant group to suppress these efforts and go back to conformity.

My Example

This stage will most likely make people around you uncomfortable because it is a very active stage. It might involve voicing objections to racist jokes, taking steps to eradicate racism in institutions and public policies, going to school board meetings, calling your elected representatives, and so on.

Your Example

Now that we understand these different stages, I want to again explain that these are not linear! You do not graduate from one stage to another. If you make it to *commitment to antiracist action,* that is not where you stay for the rest of your life. If you make it to *integrative awareness,* that doesn't mean you can stop now. You can be in one of these stages at noon and be in a whole different stage by three-thirty. Why? Because our real lived experiences are constantly shaping our identity, and the change in identity changes our needs.

Here's an example with the model.

Let's say I am feeling really good, life is good, relationships are good, and I am in *integrative awareness.* I know who I am, I am confident in who I am, and I can hold that in tandem with knowing racism is real and that not all white people are bad, and that we are all victims of the system. I truly do believe those things, but guess what? When I open my phone to find that an innocent Black man has been murdered in cold blood by a police officer and they aren't sure if any charges will be pressed, you would be out of your mind to think I am staying in *integrative awareness.* Everything in my body jumps to *resistance and immersion.* It's us versus them.

The environment, new information, old feelings— they all created a shift in where my identity as a Black woman was rooted in that moment.

Here's an example for my white friends. Maybe you have done a lot of work, maybe you were off at school studying and reading, you learned how to use your voice toward antiracism, and you are the person who calls out every joke, points out who is not seated at the table, and writes letters to your professors about adding more diverse authors to the syllabus, and then you go home for Thanksgiving. The conformity creeps back in. Your parents' house and the presence of your family pokes and prods at all different corners of your identity and the work you have done, and there you find yourself in conformity—your uncle makes a racist joke and you say nothing.

Where would you currently place yourself in this model? What was the most recent situation in your life that pushed you to be in this stage?

....

....

....

....

....

....

....

....

We all wish we could be integrated and be antiracist one hundred percent of the time, but it just isn't realistic. Even the gentlest of parents lose their cool every once in a while when their kid throws a tantrum. We don't have to feel shame about it, we don't have to pretend like it doesn't happen, but it does serve us well to be aware of it.

Think of a time when your identity development was shifted. Where were you? What happened? How did it change?

....

....

....

....

....

....

....

So why is this important? Because knowing how our identity is shifting, being aware of where we are (in all areas of life), is what helps us set appropriate and reasonable boundaries.

After I came out, I was still willing to have conversations with friends from church who still weren't sure where they stood on the "issue of sexuality" at first. It didn't feel bad to have those relationships, but as my queer identity solidified, as I watched tragedies like the Pulse nightclub shooting happen, and as I met more and more queer people who had been so deeply wounded by the church, those relationships were not OK for me anymore.

What boundaries have shifted in your life as your identity has shifted?

....

....

....

....

....

....

....

Now, is it right or wrong to have relationships with people who aren't affirming? Is it right or wrong to have relationships with people who voted for the president you hate? These are not the right questions we need to ask. We need to stop trying to find the absolutes and start asking questions like:

"For where I am right now, are the boundaries I have working, or do they need to be reevaluated?"

"If this person refuses to change and grow, what response fits best with my healing journey?"

And let me tell you right now, that answer may change, it may be different from someone else's, and that is OK.

Sometimes I have aspirational boundaries. I want to be a person who can have bridge-building conversations, but I just need to acknowledge that is not where I am right now, and that is OK.

What belief do you hold that your current version of yourself is having trouble living out?

....

....

....

....

....

....

....

We are fluid people. Our identities shift and move as our life shifts and moves. You can go years without your identity as a sister being at the front of your mind, and then your sister gets engaged, you are her maid of honor, and all the other boundaries in your life shift. Or maybe we experience a national tragedy and your identity as a queer person is front and center, and your boundaries shift in the wake of that. Maybe you just read *The Autobiography of Malcolm X* and your boundaries need to shift because of it.

What identity is top of mind for you right now?

....

....

....

....

What boundaries have you needed because of that?

There is not one right way to be a person, and there is not one right way to set boundaries, but I think we will all be at our best when we allow for who we are to flow and adjust, and when we let our boundaries do the same.

I had a friend who was going through a divorce, and her partner was crying and saying that they thought love was unconditional. We had a conversation about the reality that love may be unconditional, but relationships aren't.

Find the conditions that work for you.

If there is a specific celebrity who, every time you go to their page on social media, makes you feel rage—maybe stop clicking on it.

If every time you walk into church, you are flooded with shame and guilt—probably a good idea to stop going.

We need to give ourselves enough boundaries to find healing, because our healing is going to be the single biggest determining factor in the success of our work here as humans.

8

Charting a Way Forward

N THE LAST CHAPTER OF *DO YOU STILL TALK TO GRANDMA?* I lay out three things that we need to be engaged with if we are going to understand not only how to ground ourselves in the present moment but also how to chart a way forward.

Those three elements are:

> Remember
> Imagine
> Act

Remembering is an absolutely integral part of being present. It is our knowledge and understanding of the past that allows us to assess and understand our current reality most accurately. Remembering who we have been as we have evolved and changed throughout our lives is probably the single most effective way we can guard ourselves from the pitfalls of progressive amnesia. It can be the gut check that stops us from calling for punishments over consequences. It is what allows us to have empathy and understanding.

What versions of yourself do you need to remember to stay empathetic and present in this moment?

....

....

....

....

....

....

....

....

Remembering can also allow us to see hope in a different way. An old adage says that our job is to plant seeds for trees we will never sit under. I like that idea a lot, and it also reminds me that I am sitting under the shade of trees that were planted long before me.

Whose trees do you currently sit under in your life?

....

....

....

The second step we need to engage in is imagination. The science fiction writer Octavia Butler (I am a super-fan) showed us that all justice work is fiction writing. All of the heroes and leaders we love and admire and follow—they all had an imagination for something that was not yet real and tangible, and so they worked every day to bring that imagination to life. When Dr. Martin Luther King, Jr., talked about Black kids and white kids playing together on playgrounds—that was his imagination, a world he dreamed of. Imagination is a sacred practice for moving forward. Imagination reminds us that we are not bound by the realities of right now.

What is the world that you imagine?

The last step, perhaps the most important of all, is to act. We must act. Once we remember, we find hope, and once that hope and empathy lead us to a new imagination, we have to do something about it. We have to act on it. My imagination, the world I dream about, is a world without guns. It is the sacred imagination my head creates of kids in school without fear and living life without hearing about the latest shooting. That is the world I imagine, but if I do nothing, if no action comes with that imagination, then it was for nothing, right? We have to move. And no, it will not be perfect, and no, you are not guaranteed to see the completion of your work, but we must act anyway. You may be planting a seed for someone else to water, and that's OK. You may be watering a seed planted generations ago, and that's great too. However you can, you have to start imperfectly moving toward the world you imagine.

What action is your imagination demanding of you?

© KIANA SCOTT

BRIT BARRON is a renowned speaker, teacher, storyteller, and author of *Worth It: Overcome Your Fears and Embrace the Life You Were Made For.* Brit's ideas and accomplishments have garnered the attention of numerous prominent national publications, making her a highly sought-after speaker on the topics of sexuality, spirituality, race, storytelling, and personal development. Brit and her wife, Sami, live in Los Angeles, California, with their dog Charles Barkley and numerous houseplants that they do their best to keep alive.

britbarron.com
Facebook: britbarronofficial
Instagram: @britbarron
X: @britbarronco